THE TERM 'CROWN OF GLORY' IS
A REFERENCE TO YOUR HAIR!

EMBRACE YOUR CROWN!
IT IS BEAUTIFUL AND UNIQUE!
ROCK IT WITH PRIDE!

-TYIA LASHE

PICTURES ILLUSTRATED BY ROS WEBB
https://www.fiverr.com/luvbeautiful

ISBN 13: 978-0-9986624-9-7

Crown Silhouette Credit: https://commons.wikimedia.org/wiki/File%3ACrown_Silhouette.svg

MY CROWN OF GLORY

WRITTEN BY TYIA LASHE
ILLUSTRATED BY ROS WEBB

MY CROWN OF GLORY IS MAJESTIC.

IT'S FULL OF WONDER AND MYSTERY.

I PROUDLY WEAR THIS REGAL CROWN.

IT'S A TALE OF MY ILLUSTRIOUS HISTORY.

SOMETIMES, IT GIVES ME TROUBLE.

SOMETIMES, WE GET ALONG FINE.

MY BEAUTIFUL CROWN OF GLORY

IS TRULY SOMETHING DIVINE.

BEAUTY, GODDESS, SUPREME,

I WEAR IT DAY BY DAY.

LONG, SHORT, KINKY, STRAIGHT,

SUPERB
IN
EVERY WAY.

I ADORE MY CROWN OF GLORY.

IT'S SIMPLY ONE OF A KIND.

I LOVE MY CROWN OF GLORY.

I'M SO GLAD IT'S MINE.

DEFINITIONS

MAJESTIC- (*adjective*); impressive beauty

ILLUSTRIOUS- (*adjective*); well-known, respected, and admired

REGAL- (*adjective*); fit for a queen

DIVINE- (*adjective*); excellent or delightful

GODDESS- (*noun*); female who is adored

SUPREME- (*adjective*); superior

SUPERB- (*adjective*); excellent or impressive

ABOUT THE AUTHOR

Tyia Lashe is a Kansas City native. She believes that beauty comes in many forms. Tyia aims to promote self-love, creativity, positivity, and happiness through her literary works.

'*My Crown of Glory*' is Tyia Lashe's third self-published book! Be sure to check out Tyia's other literary works on her website.

STAY CONNECTED

Instagram: @abeautifulwonderfulme

Website: www.abeautifulwonderfulme.com

Facebook: www.facebook.com/ABeautifulWonderfulMeLLC

www.ingramcontent.com/pod-product-compliance
Lightning Source LLC
Chambersburg PA
CBHW041222040426
42443CB00002B/50